Praise for The Transformational Nature of Grief

"*The Transformational Nature of Grief* by Cara Hope Clark is a gem of a book! It's written for those in the throes of deep grief and who are experiencing "grief brain". Cara gives us short understandable nuggets of wisdom gleaned from her deep dive into her grief from the past eleven years. It's a source of respite for those who find themselves suddenly in the grief club. You don't have to do grief alone, and this book gives you a solid companion to support your journey through it. It is easy to read, written with the griever in mind, who often has a hard time reading anything. You could simply open the book randomly to receive wisdom or you could read it cover to cover. Or you could simply read the *Soul Notes* - the prompts and questions for you at the end of each section to expand your awareness into your grief or use them to guide your journaling practice."

~**Beth Erlander**, MA, LPC, She/Her/Hers,
Grief Friend, Yes Tree Counseling, LLC

"This companion to Cara's first book, award-winning *Widow's Moon*, is truly a 'A glimpse of light through the darkness of grief'. Her words radiate the strength, wisdom and personal growth this transformational period in her life has delivered. The *Soul Notes* at the end of each passage give one the chance to look deeply into their own soul experience, to dig deep to find not only the shadows but the sparks of light that are always there even when we forget. This book is a true gift of light from Cara's soul to yours."

~**Terra Lyn Joy**,
MS, CIH, TT Mentor/Coach at "Re-Wild Your Life"
Author of *Daisy & Herm - An Unconventional Life*

"*The Transformational Nature of Grief* is another insightful guidebook by a wise teacher who has lived through - and survived - traumatic loss. Sharing her wisdom gained, Hope is a trusted friend and guide for us all. None of us escapes the loss of many of those we love and we must find our path through the trauma to heal our hearts. Whether it is the loss of a beloved spouse, child, parents, siblings or close friends, the anguish can feel unfathomable. Hope provides a warm light from her reservoir of experience to support us through our dark nights. This guidebook is a balm for each of us with the awareness that we are not alone and the encouragement to do the inner work for our own healing."

~ **Lynn Pace**,
Ret. Hospice Community Outreach Coordinator,
Support Team Consultant and Trainer, Social Worker

"This book is an extremely well-written guide for discovering how grief can transform our lives and awaken our souls. Cara Hope Clark, the author of the award-winning *Widow's Moon*, provides an exquisite collection of heart-warming concepts that prompt the reader to take a deep dive into their own experiences. Discover how to recognize and embrace the healing aspects of grief to enable wellness and recovery. Multiple *Soul Notes* stimulate internal dialogue that enhances the processing of grief, transforming pain into enlightenment. I highly recommend this extraordinary 'Pocket Guide' for all those encountering the passage of loved ones. Give yourself a beautiful gift by receiving the support and illumination inherent throughout *The Transformational Nature of Grief*."

~**Rebecca Austill-Clausen**,
Reiki Master, Occupational Therapist,
Award-Winning Author of *Change Maker:
How My Brother's Death Woke Up My Life*

"Cara Hope Clark expertly weaves this guide through grief. As a widow of my own husband's suicide, I recognize the high value of her messages. As an act of self-love, I encourage anyone who is grieving to pick up this small but powerful book. Grieving is the most difficult thing for a soul on this earth to endure. The *Soul Notes* at the back of each chapter provide important reflective questions to foster growth over time. This book will support your grief journey and captures the essence of love to accompany you on the road ahead."

~ **Jennifer Angelee**,
Author of *Beloved, I Can Show You Heaven,
21 Signs from Loved Ones in the Afterlife
and Stairway to Heaven*

"This is a lesson in radical self-compassion for turning inward in order to heal after loss. In *The Transformational Nature of Grief*, Cara reminds us of the rejuvenating power of self-awareness, appreciation, acceptance and kindness we can give ourselves as we journey through grief."

~ **Jen Zwinck**,
Host of *Widow 180*: The Podcast;
Co-Founder of the *Widow Squad Membership Community*

"It is an ancestral understanding that story is medicine. In this book, Hope has shared her story while empowering you to share your own. Go ahead. There is nothing to fear. In doing so, you may find it difficult to discern whether you are experiencing tears of sorrow or joy, because they are so tightly interwoven. Both relate to an open heart. And an open heart is where healing begins."

~ **Gregory Lathrop**,
RN, Nurse Advocate for the Dying,
Elder Council member with *CCLD*
(Center for Conscious Living and Dying)

"Grief is a deeply personal and emotional journey that is unique for everyone. Life can sometimes change in the snap of a finger, shattering life as we know it. However, the award-winning author and widow, Cara Hope Clark, has written yet another award-winning book, *The Transformational Nature of Grief* that will help the grieving dig their way out of the rubble and courageously navigate back to the world of hope again, just as her name implies. I highly recommend her heartfelt book!"

~**Janet D. Tarantino**,
NDE Experiencer, Researcher, Speaker, Inventor,
Award-Winning Author of *DYING TO SEE Revelations About God, Jesus, Our Pathways, And The Nature Of The Soul*

The TRANSFORMATIONAL NATURE of GRIEF

CARA HOPE CLARK
Author of Award-Winning
Widow's Moon

The TRANSFORMATIONAL NATURE of GRIEF

A Pocket Guide Embracing the Light of Your Soul

Copyright – ©2023 Cara Hope Clark

All rights reserved. No part of this book may be reproduced or transmitted in any form or by any means, electronic or mechanical, including photocopying, recording, or by any information storage and retrieval system, without the written permission of the publisher.

The author of this book does not dispense medical, legal, or psychological advice or prescribe the use of any technique as a form of treatment for physical, emotional, or medical problems without the advice of a physician. The intent of the author is only to offer information of a general nature to help you in your quest for emotional and spiritual well-being. In the event you use any of the information in this book, the author does not assume responsibility for your actions.

Editor: Susan Nunn
Cover Designer: Pro_eBookcovers at Fiverr.com
Illustrators: Canva
Book Interior and E-book Designer: Amit Dey—amitdey2528@gmail.com
Author's photo: Steve Gaudin—www.stevegaudinphotography.com
Production & Publishing Consultant: CSUSANNUNN.COM

ISBN: (Paperback) 978-1-7371414-2-6
ISBN: (eBook) 978-1-7371414-3-3

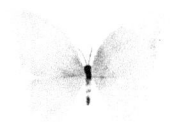

Dedication

To my son Noah who continues to inspire my own journey every day I watch his.

To you, my courageous fellow traveler. May your inner light awaken, illuminating your path through grief.

Table of Contents

Introduction 1
My Teacher 7
Suicide Loss 11
Enchanted by the Past. 15
A Powerful Presence. 19
Pool of Surrender 23
Acceptance 25
Alone 29
Sacred Breath 33
Left Behind 37
Two Hearts 41
I'm Still Alive 43
Befriending Self Love 47
My Grief 53
Conscious Choice 57

Wielding Gratitude	61
Transformation	65
Lifelines	69
Holiday Self-Care	73
The Duality Within	79
Widowhood	83
Collective Grief	87
Ten Years	91
I Remember	95
Parting Words	99
About the Author	103
Share The Love	107

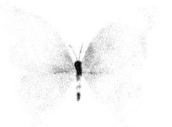

Introduction

To be honest, I wasn't expecting to publish a second book on grief. After all, I had already gone to the depths of my heart and soul writing my memoir *Widow's Moon*, recounting my own transformational journey through grief after the loss of my beloved husband Claude to suicide in 2012.

So why, you may ask, am I here writing these words for you?

My answer, though it might seem vague, is that we may not initially understand or know the answers to the whys. We just know that it's something that we are called to do. A divinely appointed dedicated action that tests our faith and resolve every step of the way.

Sure enough, this is one of those times, and I am honored to heed the call.

This book is designed with you in mind, or maybe a friend or a family member who has suffered a loss. Rather than a step-by-step guide, I use the power of inspirational storytelling as a valuable tool to assist others. I believe that when we are able to share our own stories of transformation, we are able to awaken and touch the hearts of others.

Acknowledging this, I have purposefully written new entries as well as extracted passages from previous writings such as my blog, journaling and my memoir *Widow's Moon*. Some passages are bite-sized while others are mouthfuls. All are intended to bring you inspiration, fresh perspectives, hope and solace at a time when you need it most.

The title, *The Transformational Nature of Grief*, came through as I reflected on what my own journey has meant to me. Each chapter builds on the next as I illustrate how my changing seasons of grief have led me to an elevated point of view. From this vantage point, we can begin to see that the light of our souls still shines brightly though we may feel that we are enmeshed in darkness.

In addition, I envisioned this book being used as a pocket guide of sorts. Your own personal companion, one that you can return to again and again as you feel the need. As I sat with this, I noticed yet another auspicious meaning that initially eluded me. Our soul (or our higher self) is our constant companion that we can lean on as we move through the many phases of our lives. Grief is no exception. My hope is that the words on these pages will serve as a reminder of this ever-devoted aspect of ourselves.

In the chapters that follow, I dive back into my vast reservoir of memories, allowing the wisdom and the medicine to surface. Much of what I share emerged during my seven years spent living in the peaceful beauty of Boulder, Colorado. This was a potent time of healing and transformation. While living in Boulder, I found my heaven on earth. As a Taurus, I have always sought comfort and solace in nature. It was there in the silence and serenity that I was able to tap into my inner wisdom and share the teachings that came through me.

I reflect on my own personal losses with an emphasis on the loss of my husband. I impart insights, revelations and things I have learned along the way that have been helpful and supportive. My hope is that by sharing my journey I can in some small way illuminate and inspire yours.

All of us in this human experience inevitably find ourselves experiencing grief at various times in our lives with varied intensity. We may have lost a loved one, a beloved pet, ended a meaningful relationship, lost a job, or had our dreams shattered. Often, we are caught completely off guard and have no idea how to navigate such treacherous waters. We may feel alone, set adrift, possibly even desperate, having no idea how we will stay afloat. I know that's how I felt.

Despite this, I want you to understand that you are not alone. Life does find a way and there are many opportunities to not only survive but thrive after our losses. We are on a path that is unique to each one of us, with no timetable and no destination. Though, we might yearn at times for there to be one.

My life has been forever altered. Grief has held me so deeply in its clutches that I have wondered how I could have survived it. It has transformed me to my core and taken me to places deep within that were previously unrevealed.

Grief has the ability to crack us wide open, uncovering the light-filled gifts that lie in wait for us to discover when we least expect it.

If we can make room in our hearts for these gifts alongside our grief, we can keep moving forward one small step at a time, all the while knowing we are loved and cared for beyond our wildest dreams, divinely guided every step of the way if we are willing to listen.

It has not been an easy passage, to say the least, but I can say with certainty that I am grateful for it *ALL*. I would not be the woman I am today who holds a deeper sense of self and purpose if I had not traveled on this ever-transformational road through grief.

After many years, I have learned to view grief as my sacred teacher, my soul-driven guide. It may not be possible to adopt this point of view when your heart is aching so deeply you can hardly breathe. Believe me, I get it. However, when you are ready, I invite you to "feel" into this new awareness. Allow it to seep in, nourishing a budding alternative viewpoint as you move through your own grieving process.

Our soul needs an open channel through which it can communicate with us. One of the many tools used to nurture and access these channels of communication is through journaling. As I previously mentioned, some of what I share here came from my own journal entries. To get you started, I have included what I call *Soul Notes* following each chapter. By design, these journaling prompts hold the potential to spark inspiration when you are ready to explore.

Journaling can also be a safe place to put our unresolved emotions that we are fearful of sharing with others. Especially while we grieve, we may at times feel like a broken record, and not want to burden others with the weight of our grief. You might also find that this is a sacred place to practice gratitude and set intentions.

You may want to create a ritual around journaling. To set the stage, light a candle, put on some soothing music, or go to a favorite spot out in nature. Some suggestions to assist with feeling more in the present moment might be to take a few deep breaths, feel into your body, mind and emotions, notice your surroundings and ask for spiritual guidance before you start.

There may be times when it feels like your loved ones who have passed are speaking to you through your writings. I found that this was a direct line for Claude and me to communicate. Or perhaps your angelic guides may chime in. It may seem a bit odd at first and hard to believe, but over time it is possible to begin to trust what comes through you.

Let the words flow *uncensored* to begin dreaming your way onto your new life path.

Let's face it: we all need a helping hand while we grieve. Often many hands. My hope is that mine may be one of those. I humbly invite you to step forward with me as we explore this mysterious world of grief. Will you join me?

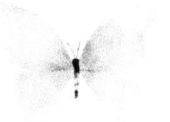

My Teacher

One of the many things I have learned is that grief is not a one-size-fits-all endeavor. Though there are many commonalities, it's important to note that my experience may be different than yours. In addition, each loss will likely activate our own unique soul-designed path leading the way to our individual healing and self-discovery.

For me, the way through has been imbued with my lifelong belief that we are much more than this human experience. We are divine beings of light living and learning through all of our earthly struggles and joys.

By holding this perspective, I have been able to see that grief has been my teacher. Grief has taken me down the rabbit hole to the transformational gateway of my soul.

Truth be told, I could not have done this deep inner work without the assistance of grief counselors and the numerous gifted holistic practitioners by my side. Each, in their own way, held me safely in the sanctity of the work they embodied.

For as long as I can remember, listening to my inner voice has been my true north. My higher wisdom in tandem with my angelic guides are always here with love and light piercing through my doubts and fears. When I am able to truly listen, I am able to shift my energy and remember that I am much more than my grief.

Soul Notes

If I were able to experience grief as my teacher, giving me a new perspective, how might that new insight inform my path moving forward?

Knowing how important support can be during this time, have I been able to reach out to others with my grieving process? If so, what has that looked like, and do I feel I need more?

Reaching out for support can feel daunting for many during these times. Despite this, can I honor that need and feel the value in doing so? What steps can I take to move forward in creating this healing path?

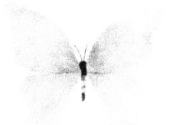

Suicide Loss

I momentarily slipped back in time. In the months following Claude's suicide, I felt I needed to protect those around me from the horror of what I had experienced. It goes without saying that the stigma surrounding suicide is another deterrent for many of us. I was hesitant to include this chapter for those same reasons. Catching myself, I snapped out of it. After all, this is my life; it's what brought me here.

Sadly, I have discovered that far too many of us are touched by suicide, some multiple times. I had no idea it was so prevalent until this happened in our family.

When we lose a loved one, our reactions are especially complex. That's a given. However, I'd like to briefly shine a light on the harsh reality that a loss by suicide is among the most difficult of losses to process. It has the consequential distinction of setting in motion a wave of grief that is torturous in nature. It can haunt loved ones for years with unanswered questions, anger, guilt, trauma and unyielding heartache.

In addition, as a society, we tend to want to keep such taboos "hush-hush". This only adds to the weight of our grief.

In my opinion, those who choose to take their own lives often don't intend to hurt others with this act. I imagine that they would prefer to stay with us. I know my husband would have opted for that alternative if he had been capable of making a rational choice. But he was living in a distorted version of reality and a world filled with unceasing pain and shame. Utterly desperate.

Suicide feels like the definitive conclusion. In other words, it's the only way out for them. In their distorted minds, I think they feel they are actually helping us by leaving. But sadly, they fail to see the bigger picture, the aftermath, the complete and utter devastation in the wake of their departure.

As suicide survivors, we need to have an abundance of love, forgiveness and compassion for ourselves, and if possible, for our beloveds who have left us. This is a monumental loss, a journey that is not for the faint of heart. It takes courage and persistence to work through the maze of emotions that evolve within us as we move along this path.

It starts with a commitment to our own selves and a commitment to life. Yes, it's true we will never be the same, how could we? Yet through this heartbreaking experience, there is the absolute potential to find ourselves growing, evolving and finding strength in places that we didn't know existed within us.

We still have a purpose.

Both my son and I have chosen to honor my husband's memory by being the best versions of ourselves that we can possibly be. I fully believe that our loved ones, who have passed, want us to be free of pain and live a life filled with love and laughter. Let's see if we can awaken the joy within us, allowing it to percolate through our lives a little bit more each day. Life continues, so why not allow ourselves to appreciate the gifts that remain?

Soul Notes

Do I have unresolved emotions such as anger or guilt around losing my loved one to suicide? If so, have I been willing to reach out for support to work through these feelings?

Having experienced a loss by suicide, have I felt able to be honest about my loss with others, or do I feel the need to hide the truth?

What do I need in order to feel more at peace and whole again after my loss?

Enchanted by the Past

While we are caught in the perpetual waves of grief we are called to go deep, to determine what we are made of. In the process, we have the opportunity to learn who we are as a spirit or soul and why we are here, always holding in our consciousness that we are much more than this personality self. Much more than this storyline that we are participating in.

We are miners digging for gold. Finding all the gems that we have kept hidden from others and, yes, even ourselves.

Grieving holds an opportunity, if we allow it, for our soul's purpose to become activated, bubbling to the surface, illuminated in ways that would not have been possible otherwise. This experience has been designed on a soul level. It serves as a catalyst to propel us into this new existence, this new way of perceiving the world and our place in it. Embrace it. Allow it to form and shape you. We must let go of all that we thought we were. We cannot go back. Holding on to the past only brings us pain and suffering; our salvation resides within the present. Right here, right now. The longing for what *was* only keeps us stuck and frozen like a deer in the headlights from what *is*.

Our memories play and replay. In desperation, we hold on to every small detail, keeping us from engaging with the sweetness that only the present moment can offer.

We can easily get lost in this memory mining. It can feel comforting at times. After all, some reflection on our past can be nourishing in moderation. However, we can become enchanted with this "searching for connection" to our loved ones through the pictures in our minds. It's as if by doing this we believe we are somehow bringing them back to life. But then we snap out of it and realize they are gone, never to return. We are left with that painful realization, leaving us with a gaping hole so vast we feel desperate to fill it. In response to this, we keep the memory replay on automatic pilot, hoping that somehow, we can slowly refill that empty space with each installment.

Here's the secret though – when we can break the cycle of our incessant memory replays then we are truly free to be present in this moment. We can grieve without the suffering. We have more space to breathe, have more space to create our new reality, our new life. We are not stuck in the past. We are alive and we are free, just where our beloved ones who have passed want us to be.

Soul Notes

Can I allow myself to take a breath and really ground into this moment? What illumination is waiting here for me?

What steps can I take today to shift my thought patterns from my past attachments to embracing the gifts of this present moment in time?

If I could hear the whispers of my soul guiding me on my renewed life path, what would it be saying to me?

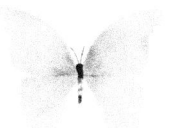

A Powerful Presence

It has been fourteen years since my mom passed beautifully and on her own terms in hospice care at the age of 83. I was blessed to be by her side when her spirit peacefully left her body. I can say with certainty that it was one of the most powerful times in my life to be with her those last three days as she prepared with deep intention to transition from this life. My siblings were there alongside me to see her off. It was clearly her time, and we supported her with our love and presence.

I know this may sound odd, but when she took her last breath, we cheered in celebration. The hospice caregivers looked a bit perplexed by this response. But we knew she was finally at peace and free from the burdens of her aging body. Of course, my feelings were mixed. Along with the joy came the deep sorrow that she was gone, and that I would never again see her bright smiling eyes looking at me with such love and adoration. I would never again be able to go to her seeking wisdom and intuitive insights during my trying times.

Mom represented my lifeline to the divine. I was born into this body through her willingness to carry me for nine months. She held for me a reservoir of love that was unbending in its devotion. She had become my greatest cheerleader. Tears flowing as I write this… It was even harder to let her go since my dad had died five years previously to this. I was officially an orphan.

But as the years have passed it has become apparent that she is still lovingly cheering me on but from the other side now. Still providing her counsel, in life and in death Thelma continues to be a powerful presence. She taught me to never give up on myself, and that we all have a core of inner strength and spiritual connection that guides us as we move through this life. Two of her favorite sayings were: "this too shall pass" and "it's always darkest before the dawn". These words have been a touchstone through my darkest hours ushering me into the light. In addition, witnessing the strength she harnessed in her life was an inspiration in my own that I will always treasure and be grateful for. I love you, Mom!

Soul Notes

Are there any special memories or words of wisdom I received from my mom or dad? If so, how are they guiding my life moving forward?

How can I honor my mom's and/or my dad's memory from this renewed vantage point?

Do I feel orphaned and alone after losing my mom or my dad? If so, how can I take the time to honor the child within me that feels alone and uncared for?

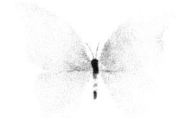

Pool of Surrender

Let's imagine for a moment if you can, that this is a deep dive into the pool of surrender. We need to give ourselves over to this experience fully and completely. It is what our soul requires and is asking for. It will accept no less than our complete and total commitment to allowing grief to have its way with us. If you can do this, trusting that you will come out the other side in one piece, you will find the true gifts that grief has to offer. What you find is up to you. But one thing is for sure: you will come out anew. The waves of emotions will tumble all the rough surfaces into a smooth flowing beautiful stone that can be taken with you as YOU!

Soul Notes

In this space resides an invitation to explore the waves of emotions that are flowing through me as I read this last passage. Am I able to acknowledge the gifts coming through as the magic of my soul and what might they mean to me?

Acceptance

One of the many self-care practices that I wholeheartedly recommend, especially while grieving, is getting regular massages. During one of my sessions, the word *acceptance* came up. When my massage therapist spoke the word, it felt like pure divine inspiration, which in turn inspired me to write these words.

What does *acceptance* mean to us on this bumpy road where grief is in the driver's seat?

For me, it's a form of surrender to what *is*. Through surrender comes peace. Through surrender, we are shown "the way". Peace is something that is inevitably lacking while we are grieving. As time passes, we can begin to feel like peace is something that will never show its sublime face to us ever again. However, in actuality, it can come in cycles giving a much-needed respite at times from the ceaseless pain. During those times, we can feel like we have found a coveted oasis in the raging storm. But, as a matter of course, we get swept away, back into the sea of despair once again.

What are we to do during these times?

Our natural tendency is to fight the current which translates into resistance and struggle. What if we were to allow the deluge of emotions to wash over us and maybe even engulf us for a time? How might that feel? In the moment, probably not so great. However, in the wake of the flood of emotions that we have not resisted but have actually invited to flow, we can find ourselves surrounded by peaceful waters, the calm after the storm.

Grieving in this way, we are not hiding from our pain, we are not clutching and holding on for dear life; we are in the flow, feeling the full force of our feelings. Honoring all that is.

You might ask: "How do I do this? I am too afraid I will be swept away with the intensity of this pain." It's incredibly challenging to maneuver through these tangled emotions that envelop us during these cycles. My answer is that we breathe, we breathe and we breathe again, we say yes, we accept, we surrender, we FEEL it and we live it!

When we can do this, we will find peace in the letting go, in the *acceptance* of what is. What shows up for us is needing our attention, ultimately, needing our love.

This will naturally take us to the next step, the next phase. Without surrendering and allowing, we can get caught and ultimately trapped in a holding pattern. This happens to all of us at times. It takes immense courage to dive into those troubled waters over and over again. It takes practice to develop trust in knowing we are always held in love. Trust that there is a way through, that we will not drown in the depths never to be seen again.

We are all held in divine love as we take each and every breath. We are never left alone to fend for ourselves. We are surrounded by oft-unseen life preservers. They show up for us in many forms, just waiting for us to reach out and grab one, two, three, or more, the supply is endless. This is another way that we can encourage *acceptance* to reside within, *acceptance* that we are not alone in this, even when it feels like we are.

So now I pose this question. Could *acceptance* be the oasis we seek while grieving? In essence, I would say yes. We may notice it interwoven with a myriad of emotions throughout our process, possibly even for many years. It could be seen as one of the many tools that we can fully integrate, supporting us during this time. If we can grant permission for *acceptance* to permeate aspects of our journey, it seems to me that this would be an invaluable invitation. The end result could elicit healing and moving forward, creating a "new norm" filled with hope and possibility even in the absence of our loved ones.

Soul Notes

Could *acceptance* be the oasis I've been seeking while grieving? If so, how can I incorporate acceptance into my grieving process?

How can I invite trust and surrender into my sacred journey through grief?

How do I experience the seen and unseen life preservers showing up, helping me to know that I am not alone?

Alone

One of my biggest fears after losing Claude, or each one of my parents for that matter, was of being alone. I would imagine that we all carry this uneasiness as humans when we are suddenly left standing without our beloved humans or pets by our sides. I would often think: "Who will be 'my person' now?" "Who will love me in the same way that they did?"

However, an ever-deepening understanding has evolved and become more apparent as I have moved through my grieving process:

> We live in an energetic world filled with illusion; the veils are thin and it's actually quite impossible to be alone. When we are born into this human form we have a posse of sorts, always loving us and always ready to spring into action when needed. Some call them guardian angels, spirit guides, our higher self, or even our loved ones who have passed. We are set for life

in that department. They are on call 24/7, we need only ask for assistance. Do I still get scared sometimes? Yup! But this faithful knowing has helped to soothe me in those times of darkness.

Soul Notes

Do I fear being alone after losing my beloved? If so, how does this fear show up in my life?

Are there ways that this fear is holding me back from fully embracing what is?

Who can I call upon for comfort from the other side, or on this one, during my darkest times?

Sacred Breath

Have you noticed how we habitually tend to hold our breath, especially while we are in high-stress mode and certainly while we are grieving? Sure, our bodies are on automatic pilot, thankfully breathing in and out each second of our lives. However, do we experience the expansive breath we truly need unless we make a conscious choice to engage with that practice?

I have typically found it challenging to be consistent with making this commitment to myself. Resistance seems to be ever-present even though I know I need a reset to help calm my nervous system.

Knowing that each of our lives has varied demands on our time and attention, it can be even more important to prioritize our well-being. I am wondering if you have been feeling that inner tug, gently nudging you to slow down and re-focus more on your self-care and healing. Re-learning how to just BE!

Even though I have slowed way down comparatively speaking, I have been realizing that I put a lot of pressure on myself to do more than is really in my best interest each day. I need to prioritize my time to recharge, and yes, maybe even take blissfully indulgent naps!

Have you ever noticed that the wind blows freely, unrestricted and unapologetic? Spirit is breathing the wind as it breathes through us. When we can let Spirit breathe us, we are in the flow.

Now, let's relate this to our grieving process. It goes without saying that we are likely to experience constriction, blocking the freedom our breath is meant to have. Did you know that on a physical level, the lungs correspond to grief in Chinese Medicine? Even more reason to be mindful of our sacred breath and allow ourselves to be breathed by this universal force that we are all an integral part of. This is a practice, and it takes time to create new habits. Please always remember to be gentle and loving with yourself as you are re-prioritizing your newly discovered center.

Soul Notes

Can I bring awareness to my breath? What are my habitual breathing patterns especially through my heartache?

What steps can I take to be mindful of how often I am literally holding my breath and blocking the flow of oxygen through my system?

How can I learn to prioritize my self-care and carve out time to just BE?

Left Behind

One cool winter night, I sat nestled in the warm aura radiating from my wood stove. I felt compelled to spend some quiet time writing in my journal. But instead, I found myself looking at an older journal entry.

This entry felt too powerful to stay hidden.

When I wrote it, I was in need of comfort at a time when my heart was aching and I was feeling abandoned, an old and familiar story that had been playing out many times in this life. Claude's suicide was one of those many moments in which that clearly came into form, but we as humans tend to experience this numerous times especially while we grieve.

There have been many times when I have felt left behind on this earth walk. Left to fend for myself in this vacant wasteland of grief and loneliness.

A sensation of being left in a stark white desert, completely and utterly deserted, panic-stricken. When will I see another, when will this isolation retreat?

This experience runs deep and speaks to the core of my human essence, my human fears, my human frailty.

We are stripped down to our core while we grieve. As if we are standing naked on those white sands. The winds of change swirling around us, as the sharp edges scrape and sculpt our skin, our entire being, as we traverse this landscape of grief.

Pain...suffering...love...the perceived illusion of the loss of love.

But the TRUTH is that we are love itself. We are surrounded by the indelible endless supply of love. Yet, as we are enmeshed in the stickiness of grief, we are blind to this.

We are born into these bodies all primed and ready to go. Little do we know what we have left behind for we have agreed to forget.

Nevertheless, as we move through our lives, we have glimpses. We have an innate knowing that there is more...

Despite this, we may spend years occupying this valuable commodity called a human body in a suffering stupor.

Why can't we set ourselves free? Why can't we simply see that ALL of this is but an illusion... ALL of this is but a stage where we are able to play out our repeated dramas.

Until we remember that we are never alone, then and only then we can turn the page. We can shift our story and begin again. Remembering the light dwelling within us.

We are living at a time in our world where we are waking up to our own divinity, to the sovereignty of our souls. My hope is that by sharing this passage, you will find a glimpse of truth in your own story. A glimpse of light through the darkness of grief.

Soul Notes

Have there been times in my life when I have felt lost and abandoned? If so, how can I hold myself in a place of love while exploring these places of hurt?

Can I glimpse the light within the darkness as I move through this exploration? If so, what do I see?

How can I unlock the light that dwells within to discover that I am love itself?

Two Hearts

Springtime brings with it the potential for new openings and new growth. Hope awakens inside my heart once again as I open and stretch my wings allowing them the freedom they need to fly. On one of my morning hikes with my beloved canine companion, Lyra, tender memories of Claude rose to the surface. My mind transported me to the times when he would say *"I feel something energetically in our hearts when we hug that I had never felt before you."* As I continued on the trail, I started seeing heart-shaped rocks, one after another. I imagined that this was his way of letting me know that he is still with me. Such sweetness in this. I miss you, Claude!

Soul Notes

What am I dreaming of as the onset of spring unfolds? How can I carry this emerging energy of new growth and let it inspire my daily life?

Have I seen signs and signals from my passed loved ones? If so, how do they make themselves known?

Do you have a special memory that surfaces as you think of your beloved? If so, how have you carried that with you on this path?

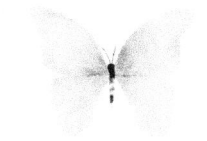

I'm Still Alive

Will you join me in this declaration?
Although my loved one is gone, I am still alive, and I need to celebrate that gift! I am still here with the ability to keep moving forward, to show up and recommit to what I came here to do. I have a mission just like everyone else on this planet.

Losing someone we love does not change that; it actually helps to shape and solidify the course of our lives in ways that we could never have imagined.

I have had this awareness through my grieving process on some level, but it takes so much time to sift through the inner rubble of grief. It takes time, and the amount of time needed is different for each one of us. It takes time to feel that it's *really* okay to move forward with our lives. It takes time to realize that we are not turning our backs on our lost loved ones by being happy or being productive people again, living a life with true meaning without them by our sides.

I know this well. I have been slowly inching my way through this, moving in that direction all along. But it's uniquely challenging to keep a consistent momentum while traversing this world of grief. Over the years I have found myself grinding to a halt repeatedly until the next round of inspiration is unveiled and I get back in the saddle.

I now recognize that it's all part of the grieving process, but it can feel maddening at times. It's a slow-moving journey that cannot be rushed; it has no time limit or timetable; it can feel seemingly endless and out of our control at times yet filled with many gifts at others.

Although I have come a long way and have created some amazing things in my life since Claude's passing, in the early years there had been an undercurrent of holding back my true joy and happiness. As if I would be betraying his memory if I were to *truly* give myself permission to live my life in a renewed way, and to fully embrace joy.

Though the pain of losing my husband will never leave me, I have been able to release the guilt that had once been stubbornly sticking to me like glue. Allowing myself to be effortlessly breathed and guided by the pulse of my life. Allowing myself the gift of freedom! Hallelujah!!!

This was a shift in my understanding of how I could truly re-create my life. There was a gradual recalibration of the old vs the new in play. This newly held belief created a fertile opening filled with hope and new beginnings. Allowing a fresh new start to awaken and bloom.

Soul Notes

In my own time, can I give myself permission to experience life in a newly inspired way despite my loss? If so, what might that look like?

> It may take hundreds of tiny baby steps, but there is no rush. Please know, your loved one would want this for you. They are by our sides cheering us on, they want the best for us. They are holding our hands through this, guiding us as we take each step that brings us closer to wholeness.

What's still holding me back from allowing myself the gift of freedom to embrace joy? What am I willing to let go of to move in that direction?

Is it possible for me to remember to always be gentle and loving with myself and adopt the mantra, *I'm still alive...*?

Befriending Self Love

I've had many years since losing Claude to delve into what Valentine's Day means to me in this chapter of my life. My conclusion is that whether I have a sweetheart or I am single is irrelevant. Valentine's Day can be a reminder to love myself up in either scenario! Of course, it sounds easy enough in theory. Sadly though, it can be challenging in our culture to truly feel unconditional love for ourselves.

Claude was not big on what he called "forced" holidays. He would rather spontaneously bring me flowers or something else to show that he loved me "just because". Since he knew that the holidays were important to me, he did both. I have to say, it feels pretty wonderful to be on the receiving end of random acts of kindness and love. I think he may have been on to something. Thank you, Claude!

Typically, when we think of Valentine's Day, we think of a day to celebrate the love we share with our sweethearts. But what if our heart has been broken? What if our sweetheart has passed on?

How can we approach this day from a refreshed vantage point, one infused with self-love and healing?

We can start by recreating and reframing what Valentine's Day looks like for us in this new reality. We could make this day about the celebration of our true essence which is LOVE. You could write a love letter to your beloved. Hell, write a love letter to yourself, you deserve it, you have been through a lot! Be generous with yourself; this is about loving and honoring all that you have done to stay afloat since your loved one has passed. Your strength, your stamina…you fill in the blank. Remember too that you were deeply loved by your beloved. What did he or she love most about you? Can you allow yourself to take in how deserving you are of love? Maybe you could imagine what they might say to you if they could write you a love letter. I can say from firsthand experience that this can be a powerful exercise if you are open to giving it a try.

You could also treat yourself to a bouquet of beautiful flowers, get a massage, take a relaxing bath, or do anything that may help soothe or bring a smile to your face. Serve up some kindness, take yourself or a friend out to dinner or a nice lunch. Take a walk out in nature. Watch a favorite romantic movie. It's okay to cry. In fact, that would be a good thing; let those feelings flow. A romantic comedy would bring some laughter and lightness into the mix, which of course is always healing and welcome.

Though it's taken some time since Claude's passing, I have been evolving and strengthening my orientation toward self-love.

In my book, *Widow's Moon*, I talk more about my experience with this. I wrote:

*"It's been an ongoing process to love myself **right where I am**. This entails accepting my human wounds, messiness and vulnerabilities, all without judgment or the feelings that I need to be 'fixed'. This human condition is a challenging quest that requires our dedicated conscious awareness. Sure, we want to heal and transform, yet we must also honor our unresolved emotional wounds and entanglements, knowing that those aspects of ourselves are just as worthy of compassion and love."*

Learning to love and honor myself continues to be a priority. Is it always easy? Nope, not at all! I have my transient dark days when it feels impossible and then the light reemerges making it easier to see the truth of who I really am: *Love itself.*

One of the many things that I have incorporated into my daily rituals is the practice of gazing at myself in the mirror.

*Each night, I look into my eyes, recognizing the brilliant divine light and love within. I smile, I touch my face and say **I love you; you are beautiful.***

In that moment, something magical occurs. I can genuinely feel universal love that transcends any emotions that I may have been feeling just moments before. I actually "feel" *in love with me!*

It takes practice to develop the habit and to feel comfortable with this. Over time, it becomes more natural, and you will experience your inner light reflecting back the love that is YOU.

You may have your own ideas. These are just a few things that I have found helpful for myself. If you need to be in your grief all day, of course, that is fine too. There is no right or wrong here. The choice is always yours to make depending on what feels appropriate.

As I write this, tears are welling up in my eyes. I know this is SO painful and challenging for many of you as it has been for me. Yet, I feel it is important to remember that love heals all wounds. Love is the answer. Love is the way through all things, including grief. If we can find a way to love and honor ourselves a little bit more each day, our hearts will mend. Our world will mend. Love begins with us. Learning to love and honor who we are in this moment and what we are going through as part of this human experience.

Soul Notes

On Valentine's Day, this day of LOVE, can I find ways to celebrate the beauty of ME?

> Think about what would make you feel special, make a list and *please* choose at least one thing to do for yourself! Remember, anything you would have given to your sweetheart, turn it around and give it to yourself. Tenderness and love and gratitude make this day about YOU.

Do I think I could give the mirror practice a try? Can I dare to acknowledge the light that resides within and love myself up?

If I feel some resistance welling up inside, am I able to explore what that resistance is about for me?

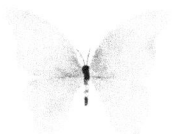

My Grief

I sat on the lovely creekside patio of the Boulder Dushanbe Teahouse one warm sunny day, with grief still securely fastened by my side. While in the company of a dear friend, our conversation took me by surprise when she asked me this pointed question: "Is grief *really* who you are?"

I thought about that for a moment and realized that in some regards "my grief" had become an aspect of my personality self or small self's identity. My whole world had revolved around it in subtle and not-so-subtle ways. Though grief is not in totality the whole of who I am, it's been one of the most potent pathways through which I have evolved and grown in this human journey. I would even go so far as to say that it's woven into the fabric of who I have *become* in this life.

She helped me remember in that moment that though this is true, I am in essence much more than my grief.

With this realization I am able to tap into a higher frequency of awareness, harnessing that which can serve to lift me up out of the darkness and into the light. Always remembering the power of my soul's path that is divinely appointed and unique to each one of us.

Soul Notes

Now I ask myself, *"Is grief really who I am?"*

Do I feel that grief has become an aspect of my own identity? If so, can I lean into the ways that grief has molded me into who I have become today?

Does it feel foreign for me to view myself as much more than "my grief"? If so, how can I see myself integrating this new perspective?

Conscious Choice

Reviewing these eleven-plus years, I have the utmost reverence and respect for the woman I was and the woman I have become. I see the magnitude of what I have faced, the strength I have harnessed and how much I have healed and evolved since losing my beloved Claude. It has not been easy. These have been the most painful and challenging years of my life. A rich path filled with darkness and light moving hand in hand, interconnected, together as one. I have learned to not only survive but thrive despite my loss and trauma.

There are many things that have contributed to my ability to heal and find peace, joy and meaning once again. I recognized early on after Claude died that I had an important choice to make. I could choose to persist with a wounded heart filled with pessimism, anger, sorrow and despair, void of any hope or meaning. Or I could choose to empower myself by learning over time what I would need to heal and grieve this loss, reclaiming and re-creating with each step. I chose the latter, doing everything in my power to heal and co-create a new life for myself and my son.

We all have an opportunity to choose at any given moment; it is never too late to change course. Without my persistence and resolve, I don't think I would be where I am today. In those many moments when I had reached rock bottom emotionally, when the pain was excruciating, I had to reach even deeper inside to find the key. The key to my existence. The key to living and loving once again. I had to recommit and affirm that I could and would get through this.

An equally important component has been reaching out to healers, therapists, etc. and creating a team of support, helping me every step of the way. I could not have done this alone. I not only gave myself permission, but I also made the conscious choice to step into my grief repeatedly full-on, head-first into the deepest depths of pain and despair. Knowing that it was required for my healing kept me going and choosing it again and again. With others by my side, I felt a safety net and the encouragement I needed to keep moving forward.

Spending time in nature has been another foundational non-negotiable aspect of my healing. I have been doing this since I was a little girl when I would spend hours out in the woods behind my family home. I have found that it is essential for me to achieve balance in my life. I have recently discovered a secluded "sit spot" that has become my special healing place. I sat there the other day taking in my majestic surroundings with my sweet little dog Lyra. I was among the "Standing Tall Ones" – the trees and mountains in all their glory as far as my eye could see. When I asked for guidance, I received this lovely message as I sat on a favorite rock tucked securely under a towering pine:

Standing tall in who we are, remembering who we are with the power of Spirit coursing through us at every moment. This is where we find our strength, this is where we find our resolve. This is where we find our peace. Through it all we remember, we remember.

We are asked to stand in our grief but usually not feeling so tall as we do so. When we can rise up to remember our soul's journey through all of these chaotic emotions, we can find our salvation even if only for a moment. With time these moments become hours, become days, become months. This can help us find perspective and understanding through this journey called life.

For me, this perfectly illustrates how *being* out in nature gives us the opportunity to slow down and remember who we are in essence. When we can allow ourselves to just BE in the quiet and stillness, we give ourselves the space we need to listen to our own inner guidance. This remembering holds another important piece of the puzzle for me, putting things in the greater context of our existence. Remembering that there is always a bigger picture at play. In any given life experience, even when it feels so unreal and beyond the scope of our imaginings, our souls have our backs. We are always being watched over and cared for. We just need to ask for help along the way. I am grateful to find continual comfort in this, carrying me home time after time on this journey.

Soul Notes

How can I consciously re-imagine my choices and my path forward?

Where in my home or in nature can I find my own "sit spot" – a place that nourishes me while exploring the depths of my healing through solitude?

I choose to say YES to love and the magic and the mystery that life holds for us all. What will you say YES to?

Wielding Gratitude

Each year, June holds the potential of being an emotionally charged month for me. Grief has revealed itself within the perfectly positioned bookends propped up by my wedding anniversary and Father's Day.

With this *one-two punch*, it's hard to avoid the emotional triggers of these two significant days. The pain of not only my father's absence but Claude's too on Father's Day runs deep. My son Noah is doing phenomenally well considering he lost his dad at the age of fourteen. But for me, this loss is unfathomable and heartbreaking. I think I will always feel that void in my son's place and for the loss of our family unit that meant so much to us.

Since many years have passed now, I have developed a rhythm and a flow in how I move through my losses. Through great trial and tribulation, I have learned to allow myself the time I need to honor and process my feelings then gradually begin to shift my thoughts and perspectives. By doing this I have given myself the authority to choose how I will proceed from that moment forward.

Please note: This is something that takes practice. Over time it becomes easier and more accessible. In the beginning, when we are in shock, overwhelmed with grief and a multitude of emotions it may not be realistic to be able to do this. But I want you to know that it is possible and can be supportive to your healing process when you are ready.

While on one of my morning walks, I was feeling heavy and sad, and I made the decision that the sadness really wasn't serving me in that moment. I felt that I needed to adjust my perspective. So, I remembered to dip into my toolbox that I have come to rely on. These tools have served to reshape my awareness, lifting me up and out of the emotional web I can sometimes find myself entangled in.

One of my favorites is gratitude. Gratitude is one of the most effective tools. When we go into a place of gratitude, we can't help but shift our frame of mind. We are able to see things from a refreshed and inspired perspective enabling us to move our thoughts in a new direction. Just one small step at a time. We are no longer stuck in the seemingly endless loop of despair. For me, this has become an integral part of my life. Without gratitude, I would be lost in the darkness with no hope of seeing the light. It does not take away the pain, but it relieves the suffering that walks hand in hand with grief.

Wielding gratitude in the context of Father's Day this year, I am choosing to be grateful that my son Noah had been gifted with fourteen truly amazing years with his dad before he left us. I celebrate Claude and the fact that he was a devoted and loving father in every sense of the word. He was fully present in every aspect of Noah's childhood. Noah received a solid foundation and developed an unmistakable sense of himself through Claude's presence. So much so that after Claude died Noah declared that he would from that moment forward take on the role of parenting himself. He would take on the role that his father had vacated. Of course, I have remained by his side. I have not vacated my role as his mom. But that pivotal decision on that day was Noah's way of taking control of the situation. He has been moving forward ever since with this premise that has fueled and motivated his life in ways that are truly remarkable. If Claude had not done his job well as a father while he was present, Noah may not have had the strong-minded determination to move ahead with such clarity and self-awareness. For this, I am exceedingly grateful!

So today, I celebrate Claude, Noah and my dad who have all gone above and beyond what was expected of them in their own unique way. I am grateful that I have been fortunate enough to be a part of their lives and a part of their love.

Soul Notes

How can I wield the power of gratitude in my life, in this moment, on this day, this week?

How can I adjust my perspective to align more with gratitude?

How can I find empowerment as I travel on this road through grief?

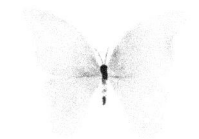

Transformation

For days now it seems that every time I look out the window or sit out on my patio, I see the graceful and seemingly effortless flight of a Yellow Swallowtail butterfly. On my morning walks, I see tiny white butterflies, sometimes in groups, that dance and fly as if they are celebrating life in all its glory. Such sweetness!

I frequently take note of the signs and symbols that appear all around us on a daily basis. The more we can open our awareness and learn from these messages, the more we start to learn that we are always being guided. That this is a form of communication from our loved ones, the Angelic Realm, God, Spirit, etc. (Feel free to fill in the blank with the language you feel most comfortable with). If we are willing to be mindful of them, they can act as beacons directing our awareness and understanding as we move through our grief and our lives. Serving as constant reminders that we are never really alone even when we feel most vulnerable and hopeless. There is always an opportunity to reach out for support.

I was in a healing session the other day and the image of the butterfly came through. The message was that the butterfly symbolizes an aspect of my own journey through grief and that I needed to honor it and its significance to me. Now, we all know the story of the butterfly and that it represents transformation, but for me, it's also a symbol of Joy. I have been inviting Joy into my life lately so it's no surprise that the butterfly would show up for me as a reminder to lighten up and dance more willingly with the mystery of life a little bit more each day.

The metamorphosis that takes place in the chrysalis is not an easy process. It is an active time, fraught with change, darkness, patience and struggle. While we grieve, we spend months, sometimes years engulfed in the darkness of our own little cocoons, struggling, suffering, processing our feelings, hopefully healing over time, trying to make sense of it all. It can be a time of deep transformation.

What holds true for the butterfly holds true for us as we grieve. We can't open and emerge from the chrysalis before we are ready. Patience and permission from within are needed to allow this process to unfold naturally and to be experienced in a way that only we can dictate. No one understands our mourning the way we do, and nobody can tell us what our journey should look like. Some people can move forward relatively quickly and others will grieve the rest of their lives in one form or another. In other words, there is a broad spectrum of how we experience and participate with our loss over time.

We all have our own individual paths to follow. There is no right or wrong here. For me, viewing this experience as an opportunity for healing and creating a new life has been in place from the very beginning. Since this road is unavoidably imbued with ups and downs, I have had to re-commit to myself repeatedly. Healing takes time, strength, tenacity, determination and, most importantly, commitment.

I am not suggesting that grief has a final destination – it doesn't. However, if you can see even a small sliver of light through the darkness and have the desire to find your own renewed purpose, I am living proof that it is possible.

It does not mean all of your pain will go away. It won't. But it will temper with patience. Yes, it's true your life will never be the same. But over time it is possible to emerge from your own chrysalis as someone who is stronger and ready to engage with the world in a way that you never could have imagined...I invite you to be open to that possibility.

Soul Notes

What signs and symbols are surrounding me in my world? What do their messages hold for me?

Am I being patient with myself as I grieve? If not, how do I see myself adopting a gentler patience in my process?

Can I feel the metamorphosis taking place within my own chrysalis as I grieve? If so, what is yearning to emerge?

Lifelines

I felt a sense of renewal after spending a week in southern California. Living in the mountains of Boulder at the time, I went there to take solace by the sea with one of my beloved soul sisters and her family, and to reclaim my connection to the Pacific Coast.

I had forgotten how blissful it is to walk barefoot on the beach with the moist sand and the cool refreshing waves caressing my feet. Each day we spent there felt like a sublime interlude. A time to pause, soaking it all in and contemplating my existence.

One day in particular I sat there relaxing on my chair, my feet buried in the soft warm sand watching the waves glistening in the sun. I couldn't help but see momentary holographic reflections of my past. Images of Claude and Noah, father and son, playing in the waves having the time of their lives, not a care in the world. Little did we know in the innocence and simplicity of those moments what the future held for us all. Who would have ever guessed that Claude would eventually end his own life? I found myself longing for Claude to be there by my side enjoying the healing waters with me. Tears filled my eyes and sadness filled my heart. Yet at the same time, I felt heartened by how far I have come along this journey since Claude's passing. I have healed in innumerable ways over these years. Those feelings of sadness were momentary, whereas in the past they may have engulfed me just as the perpetual waves of the ocean are capable of.

As a result of this trip, I became aware that for my personal well-being and continued renewal, I need the seashore just as much as I need the stability of the mountains. These are both my *lifelines*. The ocean has been important to me as a native of Rhode Island which is known as the "Ocean State" and living on the coast of Northern California for ten years. I realized a sense of freedom to reclaim my love and desire to be by the sandy shores in present time. I have now created new memories. More steps, more layers of healing this traumatic wound of losing Claude and the life we once shared.

We can lose sight, especially while grieving, of our individual *lifelines*, those things that serve to support and recharge us and help us feel our connection to our true selves. For Claude, it was the water, specifically sailing. For me it is being out in nature, basking in its endless supply of nourishing vital energy. I also need to have a home that is surrounded by beauty inside and out and is peaceful and calm. I need good healthy food and spending time with friends and family and my sweet little canine companion Lyra. I need my trusted healers lifting me up, serving as continual reminders of who I am beyond this human experience.

I have discovered that as we grieve, we need these *lifelines* more than ever. At times we can feel lightyears away from others and the slightest bit of connection to anything other than our grief. Our world can feel totally eclipsed by our pain, having absolutely no idea how to find a spark of meaning in our lives again.

Our *lifelines* won't erase the pain, but they can help us stay afloat minute by minute, day by day. They may even inspire us and illuminate our steps as we move forward with our new reality.

Soul Notes

What might my own personal *lifelines* look like for me?

Am I feeling disconnected from my *lifelines*? If so, how do I see myself reconnecting with them in a meaningful way?

What might I be able to do today to ignite or nurture those connections?

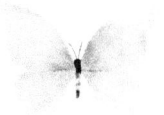

Holiday Self-Care

With each year it has become abundantly clear that making an intentional choice to take care of myself around the holidays is a non-negotiable for me.

The holidays can be a major trigger for unresolved emotions and remembering those who we have lost. Noticing the black hole in the wake of their absence seems unavoidable this time of year. Our society is practically commanding us to feel "Jolly and Bright". There isn't a lot of recognition for those of us who may be mourning a loss. Let's face it, if we are grieving, we are likely to be feeling the exact opposite of "Jolly and Bright". We may even be feeling hopelessly trapped in darkness and despair with no end in sight. So, what can we do to support ourselves through this season and beyond?

It's important to devote some time each day to recognizing the magnitude of what we carry as we walk with grief. It is an all-encompassing experience that can rattle us to our core. We must honor this process and all that it entails. To this end, I have found some things to be particularly helpful with my own grief that I will share. As a former massage therapist and energy healer, I tend to focus on self-care practices that will feel nurturing and quieting to our nervous system. But there are innumerable ways to care for ourselves during the holidays and beyond.

With holiday parties and gatherings, you may feel some pressure to be present in ways that you simply don't feel up to. However, please remember you get to choose what feels right for you. If the thought of being with people appeals to you then go for it. If you would rather have some quiet time alone, then allow yourself that choice. Please remember, there will always be those who have an opinion on what they think you need. Ultimately though, in the end, you know what's best for you. Trust that and do what you feel called to. If you decide to carve out restful and reflective time, you may want to incorporate some of the things that I have outlined below:

- One of my all-time favorites is taking pleasure in the comfort of a luxurious warm bath with candles, soothing music and essential oils to lift our spirits. This gives us an opportunity to decompress and find some meditative time that is powerfully healing.

- You could go for a spa treatment, healing, or bodywork session, maybe even include a dear friend and make a day of it with lunch or dinner included. It's so important to pamper yourself. You deserve this!

- You could spend some time out in nature, in a favorite park or outdoor space. Nature is my number one go-to for finding balance and healing. Weather permitting, I begin each day with a walk or a hike. There is nothing quite like touching the earth to help you feel grounded and gain a new perspective on your life circumstance. Mother Earth in all her glory is there waiting for us. Hear her call and take advantage of her wondrous gifts.

- You could surround yourself with a warm blanket and sit by a fire with a warm cup of tea or cocoa. You may want to spend that quiet time writing in your journal or reading an inspirational book. Or the simple act of watching the flames alone can feel calming and deeply reflective.

- Engaging in some form of physical activity is an important way to not only move your body but move your mind. Without movement, we can experience stagnation. Movement can have a balancing effect on our body, mind and spirit. You get to choose what works best for you. It could be yoga, running, walking, etc.

- Allow your emotions to come to the surface in an intentional and conscious way. Give yourself time to cry, scream, yell...whatever you need to be present with and release in the moment. You might want to give yourself some time for writing in your journal or maybe a letter to your lost loved one. Or maybe even a letter of encouragement to yourself.

- Reach out for support from a trusted friend, relative, or counselor. This time of year can be brutal and you don't need to do this alone. People may not know how to support you. The more specific you can be the more likely you will get what you need.

- When I am feeling overwhelmed with sadness, I like to put my hand over my heart. This can help open our heart center and our breath. While we are grieving it can sometimes feel difficult to breathe fully. This can help with that by bringing our awareness and our intention to our heart space and into the present moment. Equally important is to bring awareness to our ability to love ourselves in these moments of grief. So, imagine love streaming from your hand into your heart and give yourself a big hug filled with all the love the Universe has to offer!

The importance of gratitude can't be overstated even while we are grieving. Being in a place of gratitude for what remains present in our lives can feel like a soothing balm if we allow its magic to embrace us. Through a mystical partnership, our light remains shining despite the darkness, we can't have one without the other. Our souls are shining with their infinite illumination and wisdom. It's up to us to remember that even when our lives feel insurmountable, we are radiant divine beings, and we can find sanctuary within this knowledge that can usher us into a new day.

Along these lines, there is a practice where it is typically suggested to light a candle next to a favorite photo of our dear departed ones. Although I do love that idea and it is something that I have personally found comforting, I'd like to suggest an alternate version of that tradition. We could light a candle to honor ourselves and that eternal light that remains within the shadows of our grief. We could honor all that we have lost and all that we are going through by affirming that we do have the strength and resilience to get through this. Our souls are with us every step of the way, guiding us along this journey. We are never alone despite how it may appear or how we may feel in our times of deep sorrow. This simple yet powerful daily ritual of lighting a candle can serve to remind us of this.

I hope you have found these ideas beneficial for tending to your grief. They may create a respite even if it's only for a few moments during this holiday season.

Soul Notes

How can I create my own inner sanctum as I tend to my grief during the holiday season and beyond?

Of the list mentioned above, which do I feel most drawn to for myself?

How can I honor my own unique needs?

The Duality Within

As I lay awake last night with my incessant insomnia, it came to me that there are two opposing sides or fractions residing within me. There is the wounded one who still grieves her loss and expresses her needs when least expected. She sometimes needs to cry and be acknowledged that she is still alive and kicking. There are times when she needs to be nurtured and cared for. In the darkness of the night, I came to the harsh realization that she will likely be with me for the rest of my life. I have been slowly putting the pieces of my heart back together since that devastating day when my world crumbled around me. Mind you these pieces have changed and rearranged themselves over time. My life has been forever altered. This part of me still feels the loss in the deepest sense and still misses her husband and her sweet little family that they created together. She is the one who still lingers in grief. She is the one who remembers vividly what it felt like to find her beloved. She is the one who has relived that moment hundreds of times, feeling the anguish in her heart and the gut-wrenching pain.

Then there is the other side. The one who celebrates all that has transpired since Claude has left because she has a broader understanding of our life's big picture. She understands that we are all living within our own individual soul stories where we get to learn and experience all of our life's ups and downs as only a human being can on this earth plane. She knows that there is really no death, only transitions to other realms that we as humans have a limited capacity to understand. She sees that Claude's transition has served an important purpose in her and their son's lives. She understands that while this was truly the most intense and most painful experience of her life it has also been the most potent, imbued with the most rewards and gifts along its tortured and arduous path. She is filled with gratitude for the whole ball of wax. She is grateful that she has had the strength to stay alive through the many times when she wanted to give up with thoughts of suicide herself. To be alive and to be able to be by her son's side continuing to be a supportive influence is one of her most coveted joys.

Living with two opposing forces can have its challenges, however, they both hold valuable currency. She who carries the grief serves the purpose of feeling and processing her loss going deeper as time passes. Without this, there can be no healing. She who holds the message of the truth of this life holds the key to understanding. Without this, there can be no hope for the future or forward momentum, and she would ultimately be trapped in an inner world filled with suffering and hopelessness.

I now have a more conscious understanding of what these parts of me need, serving as a beacon of hope moving through the rest of my years. I will listen to my dear wounded one with more tenderness when she needs my love and support. I will also listen to the wise one who celebrates this life with *all* that it contains and holds for us. Knowing that both sides are valid and need to be held, creates a space for balance and wholeness. I affirm that I am anchoring this new facet of understanding with a heightened sense of expectation and awareness.

Soul Notes

How can I imagine caring for the wounded one within?

How can I celebrate the one who has risen from the ashes of grief serving as a beacon of hope?

What actions can I take to honor and hold both aspects creating healing and wholeness?

Widowhood

No woman ever expects to find herself donning the veil of "widowhood". We hope and pray that this particular human experience will pass us by. Yet there are so many of us who have found ourselves living within this unimaginable reality, seemingly without end.

It's been mine for eleven years and counting.

In the introduction of my book *Widow's Moon*, I share a perspective that over time helped me navigate this new terrain. I hope you find some inspiration and solace in these words:

> *Yet there are certain categories of grief. For instance, to be a 'widow' or 'widower' is different than to lose a parent. I have discovered that when we lose a life partner, we feel left alone and adrift in our sorrow. After all, we have lost our 'other half,' the person we had built our life around and devoted ourselves to. We are left alone in silence, only to ask ourselves, who am I, standing here now without my beloved by my side?*
>
> *I imagine that my story as a widow may be easily relatable to others who have suffered the loss of their*

spouse. If you share this experience, I'd like to invite you to reframe the way you regard the word "widow" or "widower". In our culture, this label can carry a negative connotation involving how we view our identity. Taking on the mantle of the widow was one of the last things that I would have wanted to experience as a woman. However, being a widow (or widower) does not have to mean we are dried up, hopeless and lifeless, ever descending into a life of misery. Our lives don't have to end when our other half's do. Quite the opposite. Over these many years since Claude's suicide, I have elevated the word "widow". I now see it as a badge of courage, signaling entrance onto a sacred evolutionary path.

Though this book is written from a widow's perspective, my journey has imparted lessons that I feel can be helpful to all those who grieve. These include learning how to hold space for grief, honoring and caring for oneself through grief, and within the midst of it all, loving and embracing one's perfectly imperfect self.

Although the loss of those you love is devastating beyond measure, it can also serve to crack you wide open in ways you never could have imagined. With your higher wisdom guiding you, you have the unexpected opportunity to reflect on your identity and the life narrative you were participating in. This season of grief holds the potential of awakening and claiming new aspects of yourself that were previously dormant or yet undiscovered.

Trust me when I say this has not been an easy road, taking me on the stormiest ride of my life. Yet looking back, it has been my most empowering and transformative journey.

If you are a widow, I encourage you to try on that badge of courage. You know better than anyone that it takes tremendous strength to keep moving forward each day, to find joy within the sorrow, to find the light within the darkness.

You have earned that badge. Grab a hold of it and shine your light, dear one!

Soul Notes

If you are a widow, how can you imagine yourself integrating your own badge of courage?

How has it felt having the label of "widow"? Are you now able to imagine a new way to re-frame your perspective?

Can you now see that this loss can also be the source of the greatest transformation on your soul's journey?

Collective Grief

It goes without saying that for all of humanity, we are living in potent times of transition, filled with unimaginable losses, changes and challenges. We may be longing for that mythical place where we felt more secure, where things *appeared* to be more predictable.

As humans who inhabit this planet, are we all carrying some level of collective grief? If so, where does this leave us and how do we move through these times? My approach has been to access strategies of self-care from my own grieving process and to look deeper into the larger question of why I am here.

Let's be curious and explore how we fit into the bigger picture. We may ask ourselves: What does this all mean for me as a soul who has incarnated on this planet at this pivotal time of transformation? Maybe then we can find a place of faith, trusting that we have chosen to be here to experience and contribute to this momentous shift.

But what about this grief that I am carrying?

Sure, when we are faced with a significant loss it can feel like the end of our world as we knew it; we can't see beyond our pain. We are in shock; we can't wrap our minds around what has happened. During these days, traveling with grief with our souls at the helm feels like the ride of our lives, a time of extraordinary evolutionary change. We have no idea where it will take us.

Just as with grief, these changing times are serving as a catalyst to mobilize us. Do you suddenly feel like you are waking up from a sound sleep, feeling awake and ready for action? If so, you are not alone. Your soul is helping you remember why you are here.

Above all else, this is the great time of awakening, to remember who we are in our true essence. Please dear one, remember to be loving and gentle with yourselves! You are more courageous than you can ever imagine!

Soul Notes

Am I following my inner guidance? Listening to the whispers of my soul, guiding me to a place of purpose and gratitude?

What am I willing to allow myself to remember about why I am here at this extraordinary time in history?

How am I being called to action, whether it be something on a grand scale or small gestures?

Ten Years

This surprised me! When I sat down to write a post to commemorate the tenth anniversary of Claude's passing, this letter to my beloved came through.

> *Dearest Claude,*
>
> *I lost you on that day to suicide.*
>
> *The shock of finding you is eternally embedded into my psyche and nervous system. Now, as I recognize this pivotal threshold, these questions have bubbled to the surface.*
>
> *What would I have thought if you told me a decade ago that I would be grateful for the transformational journey that grief would usher me through?*
>
> *Would I have believed that I would survive the pain and trauma? That I would eventually find joy and purpose again in my life?*
>
> *Would I have believed that I would eventually gain strength and wisdom beyond anything*

that I could have imagined from that vantage point?

Would I have believed that nine years later I would become an author, publishing an award-winning memoir based on my journey through grief?

Would I have believed that I would still have haunting bursts of grief from the trauma, bringing me to my knees?

What would I have said to you in response to these pointed questions? I would have screamed, "You're crazy!"

I was broken.

Over these many years, I have had to come to terms with the fact that I may never heal completely. With support and dedication, I have mended my shattered heart but recognize that this is a lifelong pilgrimage. One to be honored and held sacred.

I release the past aspects that are ready to be released and step into my future as an empowered sovereign woman, filled with bright possibilities. I am grateful to be alive as I embrace the new with a curious and open heart.

I celebrate our souls' purpose and our time together, knowing that it's all been for the highest good for all concerned. In turn, I have learned to love myself through it all, trusting that you are with me when I need you and that our love lives on.

Soul Note

You are invited to write your own letter to your beloved. Imagine what he or she might say to you about the gifts that will unfold in your grieving journey and the person you will become as you walk this path.

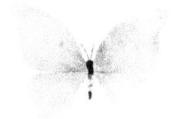

I Remember

We never know how we may feel each morning when we wake up in this land of grief. Will we feel light, will we feel heavy or something in between? In those moments when you may need a boost and feel receptive it may be helpful to hold a thought or an affirmation. You can carry it with you throughout your day like a repeating mantra. I have included these reminders as beacons of light supporting and carrying you along your journey.

I Remember

I remember
that I am much more than my grief.

I remember
to reach out for support.

I remember
to honor and express all of my emotions.

I remember
to say YES to life.

I remember
to spend time in nature.

I remember
that I am not alone.

I remember
to rest when I need to.

I remember
grief has no timeline.

I remember
to be patient with myself.

I remember
to honor and love myself for all that I am.

I remember
that I am allowed to smile, laugh and feel joy.

I remember
to follow to my inner knowing and
the wisdom of my soul.

I remember
to be loving and gentle with myself.

I remember
to be grateful, even if it's for just one thing.

I remember
that I am always loved beyond measure.

Parting Words

"Will I cling to what was, or will I embrace what is becoming?"

This is a potent and pivotal question that I asked myself many times in the years following the loss of my beloved. I'm wondering now as you read these words whether they resonate with you. If you were to pose this same question to yourself, how might this inform your new evolving perspective and *becoming* self?

I recently moved from Boulder, a place that I had once thought I would never leave. Though my soul knew it was time to go, it took my personality self a few months to catch up. Grief was alive and well once again. I grieved the loss of a place that held me so sweetly as I deepened my healing process. My connection to nature had never been so strong.

Don't get me wrong, I am grateful beyond measure. Our new home in Asheville is perched on a mountain surrounded by trees with stunning south facing views. I have nothing to complain about. Still, I was experiencing the "time between" the new and the old. A place where the "old" was no longer relevant and the "new" had yet to materialize. When we are in the transition after losing our loved one it can also feel like this. We feel disoriented having no idea which end is up or down.

As I settled in, we were approaching the winter months and I was pleasantly surprised to discover that I can see the moon rise through those unadorned trees. This felt reassuring. My reminder of the changing cycles of grief were ever present. I still had the moon to lean into.

I recognized that I wasn't ready to release my previous life, I was clinging to *what was*. At that point, I had not been ready to allow the gifts to unfold with the letting go. So I waited.

Each time I went out on my deck to view the moon it helped to anchor me back into present time. The place of knowing that I was exactly where I needed to be. A respite from the human suffering, helping me to remember that I am much more than this human experience.

I want to thank you for exploring this world of grief with me.

My greatest desire is that the wisdom shared in these pages has brought significant insights, inspiration and clarity to you, instilling you with a new understanding of the transformational nature of grief.

That you may have even discovered your all-knowing companion through the grief that resides within.

I realize that this book won't take your pain away. Despite knowing that, I do hope that these words have helped you see that you are not alone. In addition to the heartache you may be carrying, there exists the potential for hope and joy together with a renewed sense of purpose.

This is a sacred step-by-step process. There is no rushing this holy pathway.

Please remember this dear one, your grief is as vast as the stars and part of being fully human on this starship called Earth. Just like the passing phases of the moon your relationship to your grief over time will be shifting and changing. I know this can feel unsettling and may even make you feel a little crazy, but rest assured, you're not. It's simply part of your own personal passage through the corridors of grief.

About the Author

Cara Hope Clark lives in the serenity of her tree-lined perch, nestled in the Blue Ridge Mountains of North Carolina. It's here in these natural surroundings where her creativity soars, whether it be through photography, painting or writing.

Having lost her husband to suicide in 2012, she has spent years exploring grief and its transformational nature. From a path well-worn she shares her intimate path forward and inspirational wisdom, assisting others along their own journey through grief. She continues to be a guiding light as the author of this Pocket Guide, *The Transformational Nature of Grief.*

Cara is a co-author of the international bestsellers *Life Reimagined* and *Reclaiming Your Midlife Mojo;* she has been on a divinely guided personal and spiritual growth path for over forty years.

If you would like to learn more about Cara's inspirational story or seek further support, her award-winning, #1 bestselling memoir, *Widow's Moon – A Memoir of Healing, Hope & Self-Discovery Through Grief & Loss,* invites you into her deeply personal journey. In the back pages of the book, you will find her *Widow's Lunar Toolkit.* This extensive guide is filled with healing and nurturing self-care practices that will assist you on your own sacred path through grief.

Visit Cara at <u>www.carahopeclark.com</u>

Or scan the QR Code

The first QR Code takes you directly to my Amazon sales page, the second gives you other purchasing options.

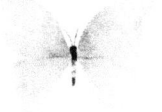

Share The Love

Thank you for journeying through these pages. If you feel this Pocket Guide would be helpful to others, please take a moment to write a short review on Amazon so that others will know there is a path forward. This small gesture means more than you know and will help me share my voice with more readers like you.

www.ingramcontent.com/pod-product-compliance
Lightning Source LLC
Chambersburg PA
CBHW071358080526
44587CB00017B/3124